Thank you for purchasing my book. Your patronage is much appreciated. I hope the book brings some joy and entertainment.

American History: Fun Facts

Visit the author's website at www.dileharris.net or contact him at leon44285@gmail.com.

This Book Belongs To:

See the following fun facts about American presidents

Did you know that John Quincy Adams used to skinny-dip in the Potomac River every morning? And if that's not impressive enough, Teddy Roosevelt once gave a speech after being shot in the chest and William Henry Harrison served the shortest term as president, catching pneumonia and dying in just 31 days into office. Who said politics can't be entertaining?

William Howard Taft weighed over 300 lbs and he had to order a special-made bathtub from a Manhattan-based company. Taft was the only man to serve as president and later become chief justice of the Supreme Court.

Joe Biden has a lifelong passion for ice cream and often shares stories about his love for it. Biden was the leading scorer among private schools in his district during his senior year in 1960. He played half-back and wide receiver.

Barack Obama collects comic books and is a fan of Spider-Man. He received two Grammies for Best Spoken Word Album of the Year in 2006.

Andrew Johnson was a self-taught tailor and made his own clothes, even while serving as president.

Bill Clinton played the saxophone on the Arsenio Hall Show on June 3, 1992.

Richard Nixon loved to play the piano and was an accomplished musician.

Calvin Coolidge had a pet raccoon named Rebecca that roamed the White House.

Dwight D. Eisenhower installed a putting green on the White House lawn.

Woodrow Wilson kept a flock of sheep on the White House lawn to save on mowing costs.

Lyndon B. Johnson owned an amphibious car and would surprise guests by driving it into the lake.

Theodore Roosevelt was an accomplished boxer and had a sparring partner in the White House.

Thomas Jefferson was a skilled architect and he designed his famous home, Monticello.

Ulysses S. Grant received a speeding
ticket in 1872 in Washington D. C. for driving
too fast in a horse-drawn carriage.

As a 21 year old, in 1830, Abraham Lincoln was a champion wrestler in his county in Illinois.

John F. Kennedy won a Pulitzer
Prize for his book "Profiles in Courage."

Warren G. Harding once lost the White House china in a poker game.

Ronald Reagan was a lifeguard during his teenage years and saved 77 lives.

Harry S. Truman had a sign on his desk
that read, "The buck stops here."

George W. Bush owns a ranch in Texas called the "Western White House."

George H.W. Bush was a fan of fast food and famously disliked broccoli.

Gerald Ford worked as a fashion
model in his youth and appeared
on the cover of Cosmopolitan.

George Washington was an avid dog lover and owned more than 30 dogs during his lifetime.

Franklin D. Roosevelt was the first president to travel by airplane while in office.

James Madison was the shortest
president in American history,
standing at only 5 feet 4 inches tall.

Jimmy Carter was the first U.S. president to be born in a hospital.

This Section is on Fun Facts about American Inventors. See the Amazing Contributions of These Great Americans. Enjoy and Maybe Learn Something You Didn't Know.

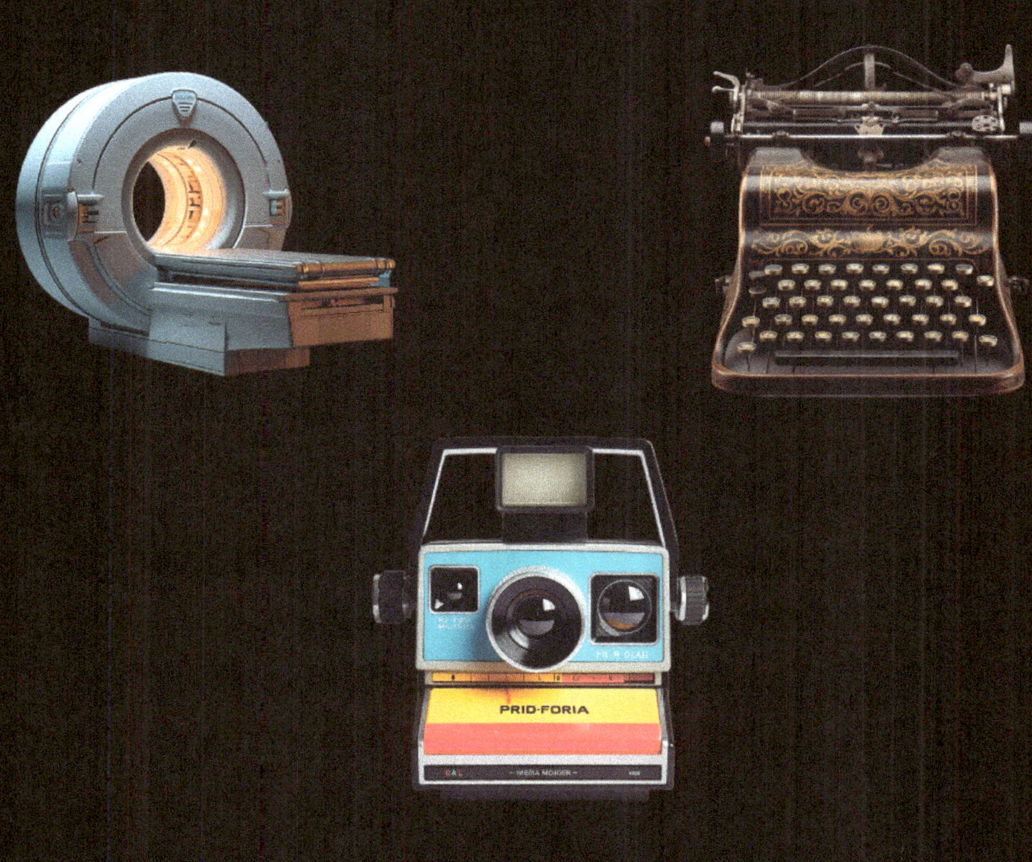

George Washington Carver: An agricultural scientist and inventor, George Washington Carver made significant contributions to the fields of agriculture and botany. He developed numerous uses for peanuts, sweet potatoes, and soybeans, including creating alternative crops to help replenish soil depleted by cotton cultivation.

Modern television was invented by
Philo Farnsworth, an American
inventor, in the early 20th century.

The traffic light was invented by Garrett Morgan, an African American inventor, in 1923.

The microwave oven was invented by Percy Spencer in 1945 after he noticed a candy bar in his pocket had melted while he was working on radar equipment.

The first air brake (1869) invented by George Westinghouse revolutionized the railroad industry.

The first practical color photograph was produced by Edwin H. Land, the inventor of the Polaroid camera.

The electric guitar, an iconic instrument in popular music, was invented by Les Paul.

The first computer mouse was invented by Douglas Engelbart in 1964.

The modern air conditioning system was invented by Willis Carrier in 1902.

Charles Broadwick was an American pioneering parachutist and inventor

The first successful steamboat, called the Clermont, was invented by Robert Fulton.

The first commercial typewriter was invented by Christopher Sholes in 1867.

The MRI (Magnetic Resonance Imaging) machine, a widely used medical imaging device was invented by Raymond Damadian.

The barcode, now used for product identification and inventory management, was invented by Norman Joseph Woodland and Bernard Silver.

The first functional artificial
heart was invented by Robert Jarvik
in the 1980s.

The first successful heart transplant was performed by Dr. Christiaan Barnard in 1967.

The pacemaker, a device used to regulate heart rhythms, was invented by Wilson Greatbatch in 1958.

Nikola Tesla: Known for his contributions to alternating current (AC), electrical systems, and his work on wireless power transmission.

Samuel Morse: Inventor of the Morse code and co-developer of the telegraph.

Benjamin Franklin: Known for his experiments with electricity, including the invention of the lightning rod and the bifocal glasses.

This Section is Dedicated to American Political Figures in American History. Enjoy Learning These Little Known Facts About America's Leading Political Giants.

Ruth Bader Ginsburg, an Associate
The justice of the Supreme Court became
the second woman appointed to the
court and played a crucial role in
advancing gender equality.

Martin Luther King Jr., a prominent civil rights leader was awarded the Nobel Peace Prize in 1964 for his nonviolent resistance against racial inequality.

Eleanor Roosevelt, the wife of
President Franklin D. Roosevelt, was
the first presidential spouse to hold
regular press conferences and
write a daily newspaper column.

Condoleezza Rice, a former Secretary of State, is an accomplished pianist and considered pursuing a career in music before entering politics.

Kamala Harris, the first female Vice President of the United States, is a member of the Alpha Kappa Alpha sorority and the first HBCU graduate to hold the office of Vice President.

Elizabeth Warren, a Senator and advocate for consumer protection, is a former Harvard Law School professor who specialized in bankruptcy law.

Alexander Hamilton, one of the Founding Fathers and the first Secretary of the Treasury, was involved in a famous duel with Vice President Aaron Burr, which resulted in Hamilton's death.

Abigail Adams, the wife of President John Adams, is known for advocating for women's rights. In a letter to her husband, she famously wrote, "Remember the ladies."

Nancy Pelosi, the first female Speaker
of the House, is the highest-ranking woman
in the history of the United
States government.

Elizabeth Cady Stanton: Leading figure in the women's suffrage movement.

Thurgood Marshall: First African-American Supreme Court Justice and prominent civil rights lawyer.

Robert F. Kennedy: U.S. Attorney General and Senator, advocate for civil rights and social justice.

Susan B. Anthony: Key figure in the women's suffrage movement.

Cesar Chavez: Labor leader and civil rights activist, co-founder of the United Farm Workers union.

Shirley Chisholm, the first African-American woman elected to Congress, ran for president in 1972, becoming the first African American to seek the nomination from a major political party.

Jorge Ramos: Prominent journalist and news anchor known for his coverage of Hispanic and immigration issues.

Henry Clay: Influential politician and statesman, known as the "Great Compromiser."

Gloria Steinem: Feminist activist, journalist, and co-founder of Ms. magazine.

Julian Castro: Former Secretary of Housing and Urban Development and Mayor of San Antonio, Texas.

Raul Grijalva: U.S. Representative from Arizona and co-chair of the Congressional Progressive Caucus.

Marco Rubio: U.S. Senator from Florida and former presidential candidate.

Henry Kissinger: Secretary of State under Presidents Nixon and Ford, diplomat, and Nobel laureate.

Jeannette Rankin was the first woman
elected to the U. S. Congress.

Al Gore was vice-president under Bill Clinton and he is an environmental activist.

Sandra Day O'Connor was the first woman elected to the U. S. Supreme Court .